Contents

	Introduction	p3
1	Tips for clear writing	p5
2	Writing for the web	p15
3	Writing email	p25
4	Jargon buster	p30
5	Writing for a global audience	p33
6	Emphasis house style	p39
7	Problem words	p57
	Index	p63

Introduction

We first came up with the concept for this book way back in 2007. My colleague Tom and I were returning from visiting some clients. It was obvious to us that their staff desperately needed a clear guide to the company's approach to written communication.

The trouble was, we knew the clients would never produce one. It was simply too big a task for them, just as it was for all the other clients we'd floated the idea with. We decided we'd better produce our own universal guide. And so *The Write Stuff* was born.

Back then, we never dreamt just how popular it would become. It's now in its fifth reprint and over 50,000 copies are in use around the globe. It's become the go-to guide to better writing for a huge number of organisations.

This edition contains the same solid advice as previous versions and a full section aimed at settling arguments about contentious spellings and points of grammar. You'll also find indispensable chapters on email, web content and writing for a global audience.

As always, we'd love your feedback on how you're using this guide and to hear about the particular challenges you face when writing in the workplace. We're here to help.

Rob Ashton
Emphasis founder and CEO

The most valuable of
all talents is that of never
using two words when
one will do.

Thomas Jefferson

1

Tips for clear writing

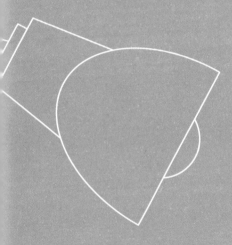

Faced with a looming deadline, doing anything other than diving straight in can feel like a waste of precious time. In fact, many people get quite self-conscious about planning, as they're afraid their colleagues or line manager will think they're not working. (Delegates often tell us this on our courses.)

But, as the saying goes, to fail to plan is to plan to fail. Never think of the time you spend planning as wasted: it is a vital part of the process.

Know your reader

We are all prone to becoming trapped in our own little world of 'getting the document done'. Yet writing that doesn't consider the reader is unlikely to succeed in its objectives, or even be read at all.

To ensure you get your message across, ask yourself why you're writing, what you're trying to say and to whom you're saying it. Make sure you are clear about what action you want your readers to take once they've read the document. In this way, you'll tell them what they need to know, not what you've found out.

Know what you want to say

You need to put your important messages at the start, so make sure you know what they are before you begin writing. Test them out loud before you commit them to paper: if you can't make sense of them, how will your readers?

We waste a lot of time crafting sentences only to cut them (or have them cut) at the final edit. So it makes sense to sort out your thinking at the planning, not the writing, stage. Marshal your material in a way that is logical and transparent to your reader. And use subheads to show readers at a glance how your themes develop.

Reader-centred writing

Ask yourself:

1 Why am I writing this?

2 Who is it for?

3 What am I trying to say?

How to say what you mean

You may want your work to be noticed, but your writing shouldn't be. In business, good writing is invisible. You have failed if you force your reader to concentrate on the words rather than the message.

There are specific ways in which you can hone your writing style to highlight what you're saying rather than how you say it.

The central readability principles are:

* be direct

* use the active voice

* keep it short and simple (KISS)

* stick to one sentence, one idea

* proofread it.

The following pages examine each of these principles in turn, and give before-and-after examples showing the pitfalls in context.

Be direct

Be direct by addressing your readers as 'you' and referring to yourself, the writer, as 'we' or 'I' wherever possible. For example, in place of: 'The writers of this sentence advise readers to adopt this technique,' write: 'We advise you to adopt this technique.' This will make your writing – and its relevance – easier to understand. 'You' and especially 'we' also make writing sound more confident, more transparent and more personal.

Make sure, too, that you write about what concerns your readers rather than about your organisation's internal processes.

Before	☆ After
Delegates are instructed to send in examples of their writing before training courses. The office manager receives the samples and sends them to the trainers, who analyse them to get a better idea of where delegates' strengths and weaknesses lie.	Please send us an example of your writing before the course. We will analyse it so that we can give you an idea of where your strengths and weaknesses lie.

Use the active voice

Using the active voice more often is the single biggest thing that will give your writing a bit of oomph. If a piece of writing seems unspeakably dull, it's probably because the writer has overused the passive voice.

Consider this sentence:

Allowances were made by the trainer for late arrivals.

This sentence is in the passive voice. The person or thing doing the action ('the trainer') follows the action ('were made').

The active voice puts the 'doer' – in grammar terms, the *agent* – first. This makes the sense clearer and the wording less clumsy:

The trainer made allowances for late arrivals.
Or
The trainer allowed for late arrivals.

You could also write the passive sentence like this:

Allowances were made for late arrivals.

This sentence doesn't tell you who took the action it describes (there is no agent). This is because, unlike the active voice, the passive allows you to remove the agent. So if a sentence leaves you asking 'By whom?', it's passive. This is why the passive may produce opaque text. Using the active voice forces you to be more specific and, again, more confident.

Before

It was assumed by management that the changes to working practices had been implemented.

 After

Managers assumed that staff had implemented the changes to working practices.

 Or

Managers assumed staff had changed their working practices.

Keep it short and simple (KISS)

Make sure you write what you mean by saying it aloud. As far as possible, use everyday language – the kind of language you use when you talk – to get your message across to your reader.

Be rigorous in your editing. Are you using the best word for the job? What do you mean? Is there a simpler way to say it? When you think you've finished, try cutting the content by a third.

Using jargon is fine for an internal or expert readership, provided you're certain they'll understand it. But avoid it when writing for external or non-expert readers. Keep abbreviations and acronyms to a minimum. And explain them when they do crop up.

Use verbs (which express actions) rather than nouns (which refer to things, people and places): it's the verbs that make language dynamic. Be especially vigilant for those heavy nouns ending in -tion or -sion, eg recommendation.

Such *nominalisations* (nouns created from verbs) can make your writing clunky and boring to read, as they attract redundant words. See the table below for some examples.

And use concrete terms rather than abstract (or meaningless) generalities: 'Help with giving up smoking' rather than 'Strategies for smoking cessation' (the title of a leaflet we found in a local pharmacy).

	Verb		Nominalisation
Use	implement/do	*not*	undertake the implementation of
	consider/think about	*not*	give consideration to
	complete	*not*	achieve completion of
	decide	*not*	reach a decision
	recommend	*not*	make a recommendation to

Before

The aim of this document is to provide an outline of systemic operations to facilitate the implementation of methodology that will assist the team in the avoidance of inconsistency in the wording used in training materials.

 After

This document outlines how we can be consistent with the wording we use in training materials.

Use the *Jargon buster* on page 30 to make sure you don't slip into management-speak or woolly wording.

One sentence, one idea

Keep your sentences short. Your reader will find it easier to understand what you're saying if you stick to one idea per sentence. If you write a long sentence, with many asides and qualifying clauses (like this one), your reader will find it hard to catch and then follow your drift and will probably have to return to the beginning of the sentence in order to make sense of it and in turn – and perhaps most importantly – act on it.

Aim for an average of 17 words per sentence; use a maximum of 35. But varying your rhythm is key: try inserting the odd two- or three-word sentence for impact. It's easy. And it may well keep your reader awake.

Before

Whilst the organisation currently relies on sponsorship from small enterprises and individuals, the cooperation of large corporate bodies, without whose funding we will not be able to provide the services our clients require, is now essential if we are to campaign successfully for legislative changes that will improve the lives of many sectors of the population.

☆ **After**

We need funding to lobby for legislative changes that will improve people's lives. At the moment, we rely on sponsorship from small enterprises and individuals. But this is not enough. Financial support from large corporate bodies is now essential if we are to provide the services our clients require and successfully campaign for change.

Keep an eye on paragraph length, too. Try to stick to one main point per paragraph. If you can't sum up that point in a few words in the margin, you've probably tried to cram in too much information.

Check it!

Proofreading isn't an optional extra: make time for it. Try to create some distance between writing the document and proofreading it. Print it out and come back to it when you're fresh. And try to proofread away from your desk – this will help you read as a reader, not as the writer. Use a ruler to guide you, and a pencil to point to each word individually. This will stop your brain reading what it expects to see rather than what's actually there.

Ten top tips for writing well

1. **Know your reader.**

2. **Know what you want to say.**

3. **Be direct.**

4. **Use the active voice.**

5. **Keep it short and simple (KISS).**

6. **Stick to one sentence, one idea.**

7. **Keep paragraphs short.**

8. **Use subheads that summarise the content.**

9. **Edit, then edit again.**

10. **Proofread on hard copy, and when you're fresh.**

Get rid of half the words on each page, then get rid of half of what's left.

Steve Krug

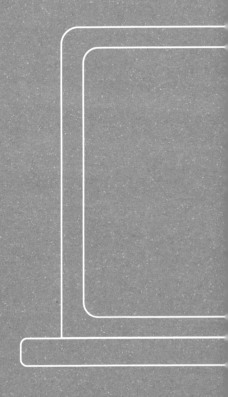

2
Writing for the web

Your visitors are on your web pages for a reason. This can range from a highly specific goal, such as to buy a particular product, to a vague need for distraction.

You need to work out which of your readers' goals also benefit your organisation, then tailor your website to meet them. As a web writer, your challenge is to make it as easy as possible for readers to find what they're looking for. Here's how.

First things first

There's a lot of information out there already. Do you *have* to write this page? Is the material already there on a different page on your site? Can you link to it to avoid duplicating effort?

Once you have considered these questions, work out how many pages you need to convey your information. Stick to one topic per page. And make sure each page is self-explanatory and self-contained. It should stand as an 'island' of information: your reader should be able to access it from anywhere and understand it.

Visitors from everywhere

Website visitors might come through a search engine, social media, a reference from a friend, a link from a site, or by directly typing the address into their browser after seeing an advert. Or they might remember your site from a previous visit.

You have no way of telling for sure where the next visitor will come from, and no control over which page they see first. What's worse, many of them will be seeing your site for the first time. They may not know how much trust to put in it.

They're likely to be asking themselves: 'Am I in the right place?' So each page needs to answer that question – and answer it within about five seconds.

This is a hard test to pass. Try it: ask someone who isn't familiar with your website to look at an important page. After a few seconds, ask them what they think that page is about. There's a good chance you'll be surprised by their answer.

If this all sounds too painful, try it on the sites of your competitors or similar organisations. You'll be amazed at how many of them fail.

Know your audience

Apply the same reader-centred approach as for printed writing. If anything, be even more rigorous. Imagine who is likely to be visiting the site – what they like, what their attitudes are and what they're looking for – and keep these typical visitors in mind with everything you write for the web.

Remember that visitors to your site may speak English as a second language. Avoid complex language, idioms, metaphors and cultural references unless you're sure that most of your audience will understand them.

Subheads and layout

Initially, visitors are much more likely to scan your website content for keywords, rather than read each page from beginning to end. Once they know they're in good virtual hands, they'll be more inclined to slow down and read properly.

You can take advantage of this by using regular, clear subheads that break up the text and make it easy for your reader to jump to the appropriate section.

Be sure also to make your subheads explicit, rather than using bland, general wording. So '40 years in the business' is better than 'Our experience'. Combined, your subheads should tell the story.

Give your writing room to breathe. Just like printed text, your web content needs plenty of space around it to make it look attractive and help it stand out.

Put the most important points near the beginning. This applies at every level: the most important message at the top of a page, the most important sentence at the beginning of a paragraph and the most important bullet point at the top of the list.

Hyperlinks

Hyperlinks within your own site can provide relevant context. They're particularly useful if you have a topic that you want to cover in more detail without crowding a page. (But remember that having too many links within your own site is distracting.)

Links to other sites can also provide useful content for your readers. But bear in mind that if you send your visitors to another site, they may not come back to yours. Make links to other sites open in a new window to help stop visitors from losing their thread.

Make sure, too, that you have real content on every page: relegating everything to a hyperlink is both irritating and time-consuming for the reader. Format hyperlinks as text, rather than ugly URLs, and use a style that underlines them or highlights them in a different colour, so readers know they can click on them. Your links should be descriptive: avoid using 'click here'. Write instead something that describes the page you're linking to, such as 'send us a message'.

Punctuate around the hyperlink in the same way as you would any other piece of writing.

— Paragraphs
— Keep up to date
— Get to the point

Paragraphs

Keep paragraphs short. A wall of text will make the reader think they have to read all of it to understand your point – making them more likely to give up. Use subheads (see page 18) to signpost content more often than you would in hard-copy documents.

Keep up to date

Review your pages regularly, making sure any dates, eg events, are updated. Out-of-date information will undermine the content of your whole site.

Get to the point

Don't mess around with background and waffly welcomes.

Get rid of any 'We have written this page to help you ...' stuff. Use the readability techniques in this guide to write concise, unambiguous text. Pay special attention to sentence length: if in doubt, put that full stop in.

Writing for social media

Social media platforms vary enormously. They're usually much more visual than the average web page – often allowing readers to see large preview pictures accompanying your writing.

But the same principles apply. And whether you're writing a tweet as the President of the United States or posting a blog update to LinkedIn, good writing focuses on the needs of its readers.

So keep them in mind from the beginning. Ask yourself what your update will mean to them.

Why will they be interested? What goal are you helping them achieve?

Not sure if you need hyphens in numbers, ages and fractions? Solve that problem here: http://bit.ly/1YhUgNm

140   Tweet

Web writing that doesn't work

This extract is from the building standards page of a (fictitious) local council website.

Before

> www.filtoncouncil.gov.uk/buildingstandards.html
>
> Dangerous structures and public safety
>
> Building Standards has a responsibility to deal with dangerous buildings as they occur. Buildings may become gradually dangerous due to old age, deterioration or settlement, or by more dramatic causes such as storm, explosion, fire or impact by vehicles. All buildings that appear to be dangerous should be reported to the Council who will treat the matter with the utmost urgency.
>
> If it is considered that a building is immediately dangerous, Building Standards can require immediate evacuation and require, or take, any action necessary to protect the public and adjacent property. Such action may involve temporary road closure, barricading, shoring, scaffolding, repairs or demolition.
>
> Where the building is not immediately dangerous, the owner would receive a notice requiring the property to be made safe within a stated time and, if satisfactory action is not taken, an Enforcement Order may be issued. If this is not complied with, the Council can instruct all necessary works to make the building safe and recover expenses from the owner.
>
> It is often possible to discuss a dangerous building with its owner in the hope that the matter can be resolved quickly without the Council instructing work on a private property.

This page hasn't been written with the reader in mind: there's unnecessary background detail and it doesn't make clear at the start what the main message is. Without subheads, it is also difficult to follow the logic.

The language is not as direct (see *Be direct*, page 8) and active (see *Use the active voice*, page 9) as it could be. And there are no contact details, which undermines the practicality of the page as a whole. Here's a rewritten version that gets to the point, signposts the information clearly and tells readers all they need to know.

 After

○ ○ ○ | ⟳ www.filtoncouncil.gov.uk/buildingstandards.html | Q

Dangerous structures and public safety

If you think a building is dangerous, please report it to us in the Building Standards team and we'll treat the matter as a priority.

Legal powers
We can often discuss a dangerous building with its owner and resolve the matter quickly. But we also have legal powers to take action to make buildings safe.

The action we take will depend on how dangerous the building is. If it's not immediately dangerous, we will send a notice to the owner, requiring them to make the property safe within a stated time. If the owner doesn't comply with initial requests, we may then issue an Enforcement Order.

Emergency measures
We will evacuate the building if we think it is immediately dangerous. We may also take other actions to protect the public. These may include temporarily closing the road, or barricading, shoring, scaffolding, repairing or even demolishing the building – recovering expenses from the owner where necessary.

Contact us
Call us on 08457 654321 or email buildingstandards@filton.gov.uk.

True eloquence consists of saying all that should be, not all that could be, said.

François de La Rochefoucauld

3

Writing email

Many of the 'rules' of email usage rely on common sense and are, to some extent, idiosyncratic: we all have our own favourite methods for structuring, prioritising and archiving messages. Here's how to get the most out of email – and ensure your reader actually reads your messages.

Is anyone there?

Unbelievable as it may seem, not everyone checks their emails every five minutes. Don't fret over a lack of response until you have genuine cause to do so.

If you simply can't wait any longer for a response, pick up the phone.

Calm down

Email is unforgiving. Without facial expression and tone of voice, it's very easy to get it wrong. What you thought was a pithy, to-the-point message might come across as terse, bossy, or – worse – aggrieved. Emails are generally ill-suited to emotive subjects: if you want to criticise or ask for a pay rise, do so in person.

Take your time responding to messages that anger or upset you. Remove the recipient's address before you write anything, so you don't send it prematurely. And save your reply as a draft to re-read later when you've calmed down.

Also be aware that successful humour onscreen takes careful thought and knowledge of your recipient. If you don't have time for either of these, keep it straight. (See also *Quality control*, page 29.)

Add attachments first

We've all done it: sent a message with attachments – without the attachments. Try adopting this routine for every message you send:

1. **Add the attachment(s).**

2. **Write the message.**

3. **Add the subject line.**

4. **Write the recipient's address.**

It's very simple, but it does work. Without an address, the message isn't going anywhere. And if you always add the attachments first, you'll be less likely to forget them. With 'Reply to' messages, try deleting the recipient's address before starting at number 1.

Use a meaningful subject line

Reel in your recipient with a relevant, unambiguous subject line. For example, 'Needs answer today' will probably provoke a quicker response than 'Information request'. Asking a question will often get a speedy reply, as the recipient feels they can give a brief answer before getting on with other more complex emails or tasks.

Remember to re-title a message that you've been batting to and fro, to make it relevant to the particular point in that message. For the same reason, give new subject lines to messages that have been forwarded endlessly and no longer have any relevance to the original title.

- Be professional
- Emoticons and emojis
- Keep it snappy

Be professional

Email has dispensed with much of the formality of traditional business writing. Using 'Hi' or just the recipient's first name then 'Kind regards' or 'Many thanks' keeps the tone direct and approachable. But beware of being too informal, especially across cultures or with recipients in a superior position. For a first contact, err on the side of caution, eg use 'Dear' rather than 'Hi'. You can always become less formal when you become more familiar with their preferred style.

Emoticons and emojis

Used in friendly, informal correspondence, the occasional emoticon (such as :-) or :-( ) or emoji (such as ☹ ☺) can serve a useful function, given how difficult it can be to hit the right tone in emails.

But use them with anyone you don't know or in more formal correspondence and you run the risk of looking unprofessional – even childlike (especially with emojis). Some people object to emoticons and emojis even in the most informal writing. If in any doubt, leave them out.

Keep it snappy

Use the KISS principles (see *Keep it short and simple*, page 10) to keep the content concise. And try to restrict the body of the message to one computer screen's length. Remember your email could well be read on a mobile device, where it will look even longer. If you can't keep it that short, use subheads or put the bulk of the information in an attachment, which you can then format in an easy-to-read way.

Quality control

Try sending your email to yourself. Oddly, reading a message in your own inbox puts you more in the frame of mind of the reader. This is a useful trick for monitoring your tone and spotting out-of-place remarks – especially when proofreading emails on a smartphone or tablet.

Try also pointing at every word onscreen with a capped pen. Read each word, one by one, as your pen points at it. This will slow you down, preventing you from jumping over mistakes.

As with all writing, try to leave some time between the writing and the proofreading of the message. If it's crucial that your email is absolutely error-free, print and proofread it before you send it (see *Check it!*, page 13).

And don't SHOUT!

Avoid writing in upper case: it's IRRITATING and unnecessary.

Remove the recipient's address before writing a reply, so that you don't send it prematurely. See *Calm down*, page 26.

4 Jargon buster

Here's a list of clichés, jargon and management-speak that we advise you to avoid, with their alternatives.

Jargon	Alternative
add value to	**improve**
adjacent to	**next to**
as to	**about, on, of** (often redundant)
at an early date	**soon**
at this moment in time	**now** (often redundant)
bottom line	**most important thing, main point**
deliverables	(Avoid: say what they are, eg **results** or **reports**.)
engage with	**talk to, contact**
going forward	(Usually redundant: rarely does life go backward.)
in close proximity to	**near**
in the case of	**with**

Jargon	Alternative
in the field of	**in**
is able to	**can**
joined-up	(Avoid.)
leverage (vb)	**make the most of** (in non-financial context)
on an ongoing basis	**regularly, periodically, continually**
on occasion	**sometimes**
outside of	**outside**
prior to	**before**
step change	(Avoid. What is the change? What does it mean?)
utilise	**use**
with respect to	**about**

Simplicity is the ultimate sophistication.

Leonardo da Vinci

5

Writing for a global audience

There's more to writing for a non-British reader than making decisions about whether to use UK or US spelling. (We use UK; see *Problem words*, page 57, for more on spelling.) This chapter offers a few tips on how to write for a global audience without confusing or irritating your readers with unfamiliar words, concepts or references.

Avoid abbreviations and acronyms

Any collection of letters may have a different meaning in other countries. So while the BBC means the British Broadcasting Corporation to UK readers, it may also stand for the Bat-lovers of British Columbia. Or the Boy Buglers of Canberra.

Use abbreviations or acronyms sparingly with a global audience and always explain them in full the first time you use them.

Be careful with colloquial expressions and popular culture

Don't make assumptions about your reader's familiarity with a particular country's culture. Many readers will have no idea what to do if you ask them to keep their eye on the ball, give you the nod or push the envelope. Nor might they be familiar with being in the black, piggy banks, ivory towers or sacred cows. Avoid such expressions.

Explain local business terms

Explain terms such as redundancy ('retrenchment' in South Africa), downsizing or brainstorming. Or avoid them altogether.

Don't talk about the weather!

Avoid talking about seasons at all, never mind whether they're particularly hot, cold or wet. Your summer is someone else's winter. And 'the hot summer of 2018' will mean very little to most of the globe. Refer to specific months instead.

Use simple language

Always go for the clearest option when choosing which words to use. Avoid phrasal verbs, eg turn up. So, ask if she came to the meeting, not if she turned up. And apply the KISS principles (see *Keep it short and simple*, page 10), using concrete terms rather than waffly abstracts.

Before
We need to think outside the box on this one and come up with transitional operating procedures so that we can put this project to bed asap.

 After
We need to be more efficient so we can finish the project by Friday.

I try to leave out the
parts that people skip.

Elmore Leonard

6

Emphasis
house style

In English, some aspects of punctuation, spelling, grammar and layout often come down to a style choice rather than a rule that everyone can agree on.

Yet you still need a consistent voice across your organisation, which is why many have a house style. If yours doesn't, you can use this chapter as a guide to best practice in modern business communications.

A. Layout

Headings

Think carefully about 'signposts' – such as section heads and subheads – because these give readers an immediate overview of your arguments and help keep them reading. Make sure the subheads actually say something about the content. Work out the hierarchy before you start, so that your main heads, section heads and subheads are consistent in size and style.

White space

Sometimes it's not what you include but what you leave out. In fact, white space – areas where there is no print, such as margins – is a key part of design. A document with wide margins, clear type and decent spaces between the lines is much easier to read than one crammed full of text.

Fonts

Some fonts – by which we mean a set of letter or number characters with the same design – are more appropriate for certain documents than others.

Serif fonts have twiddly bits at the ends of characters and give a document a traditional feel. Examples include Times New Roman, Cambria and Garamond.

Sans serif fonts, such as the one in which this paragraph is written, have no twiddly bits and lend a more contemporary air. They're easier to read onscreen and are particularly good for titles and subheads. Examples include Arial, Calibri and Helvetica.

Bullets

Use a consistent style across your document. For example, we use circular bullets in this guide.

Introduce bullets with a colon. When each bullet completes the sentence started by the introductory line, use:

* lower case
* no punctuation
* a full stop after the last bullet if it ends the sentence (as this one does).

Sometimes bullets form a simple list, where each item is only a short phrase or a few words – a bit like a shopping list. Here, you don't need a final full stop after the final bullet:

Proofreading essentials

* *pencil*
* *ruler*
* *style guide/dictionary*

— Bullets

— Tables

— Extracts

— Bold and underline

Here are our remaining recommendations:

* When each of your bullets is a full sentence, begin with a capital letter.

* Bullets that are full sentences should end with a full stop.

* Don't mix fragments and full sentences in the same list.

* Indent sub-bullets under the main bullet.

  * At Emphasis, we also make our sub-bullets smaller and black.

Tables

Also decide on a format for tables. Ours, for example, looks like this:

Table header	Table header
Table text	Table text
Table text	Table text
• Table bullet	• Table bullet
• Table bullet	• Table bullet
Table text	Table text

Caption style: make sure each figure/table has a caption like this.

Extracts

Indent quotes or extracts of more than 50 words. Don't use italics in this case, as it makes them hard to read. Introduce them with a colon (see *Colons*, page 51).

Bold and underline

Use bold for headings and subheads. Avoid using bold to highlight words within text.

Avoid using underline – either in headings or to emphasise a word.

Italics

Use italics for:

- books, publications, newspapers and radio and television programmes, eg *Troublesome Words* by Bill Bryson, *The Times*

- foreign phrases that are not assimilated into English (including Latin terms), but use the English alternative whenever possible

- emphasis in text, but use sparingly and try to find an alternative expression if possible: 'style *does* matter' or 'but style matters'

- cross-references.

Don't use italics for brand names, except where the brand name is also a publication, eg *The Write Stuff*.

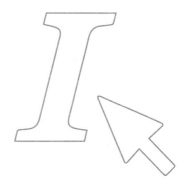

B. Names and numbers

Company names

Use the full name of a company, including the 'Ltd' if it has one, in legal/contract documents only. For general documents, refer to the company as it refers to itself.

Emphasis trainers are the best in the business.

If a company's name starts with a lower-case letter, you can replace it with an upper-case letter to aid clarity. For example, we spell Emphasis with a lower-case 'e' in our logo but nowhere else.

Capitals

Avoid unnecessary capitals, but stick to the following guidelines.

Job titles and departments

Use lower case for the general and where the term is being used as a description. Use upper case for the specific and where the term is serving as an actual title:

The trainers are busy.

All trainees will be allocated a line manager.

The chief executive is Jane Brown and the associate director is Paul Woods.

Chief Executive Jane Brown and Paul Woods, Associate Director, were both late.

Send an email to Learning and Development.

Governments

Governments are lower case if you're talking about them in a general sense, but upper case if you're referring to a particular administration:

The Government announced the abolition of the 50p tax band.

Representatives from governments across Europe were united.

Regions

Countries, states and regions regarded as having a distinct identity need capitals: France, Northern Ireland, West Virginia, the South East.

Areas that don't have a distinct identity don't need capitals: the south of Norway, western France.

Addresses

Use open punctuation – don't punctuate addresses:

Mr R Smith
Emphasis Training Ltd
130 Queen's Road
Brighton
BN1 3WB

Likewise, don't put a comma after salutations and valedictions:

Dear Mr Smith
Dear Fiona
Kind regards

Writing numbers

Write out numbers one to ten in words.

Use figures for 11 and above: 11; 61; 11,000.

Write out first, second, third etc in full (not 1st, 2nd, 3rd).

Always use figures if decimals or fractions are involved: 6.25 or 6¼.

But write fractions below one in full and hyphenate them: two-thirds of the job.

Avoid mixing words and figures in the same phrase:

You can order in multiples of 9, 12 or 16 (not 'nine, 12 or 16').

The length ranged from ¼m to 6¼m (not 'quarter of a metre to 6¼m').

Thousands, millions and billions
Use a comma for four digits or more (but not in dates): 5,000 years; 5000BC.

Write thousands as 60,000 (not 60K).

Write millions as 60 million or 60m (not 60,000,000).

File sizes should always be written as abbreviations: 45Kb, 1.8Mb.

A billion is a thousand million (1,000,000,000), not a million million.

Write billions as 6 billion or 6bn (not 6,000,000,000).

Percentages

Use 'per cent' in running text (as opposed to tables etc), not the % sign:

A good 95 per cent of delegates leave satisfied.

Almost all delegates (95 per cent) leave satisfied.

Date, time and range

Write dates in this format: 7 September 2018.

The meeting is on 8 March 2019.

Use these forms rather than the 24-hour clock: 9.30am, 5pm.

Don't write 12pm and 12am: these frequently cause confusion. Instead, write 12 noon and 12 midnight.

Use twentieth century, not 20th century.

Use from/to, between/and or X–X. But don't mix and match:

from 9am to 5pm

between 9am and 5pm

course time: 9am–5pm.

(Note that the dash is an en-rule, not a hyphen: see page 52 for more on dashes.)

If spanning dates in the same century, drop the first two digits of the second date: 1967–69.

But keep them if the dates span different centuries: 1999–2008.

Don't use apostrophes for collective dates: 1990s (not 1990's).

C. Punctuation

Abbreviations and acronyms

Don't use full stops in abbreviations or acronyms (abbreviations that can be pronounced as words). For example:

ie, eg, etc, am, pm, ltd, UK, US, Dr, Mrs, m, kg, km, Ofcom

Write abbreviations that are pronounced as individual letters – such as BBC and CEO – all in upper case. Write acronyms – such as Unicef – with only an initial capital letter.

Precede 'eg' and 'ie' with a comma, eg as in this example, or with a bracket (eg as shown here).

Don't use a comma or colon after 'eg' or 'ie':

To find out more, enrol on one of our courses, eg High-impact writing.

Don't use apostrophes to make abbreviations plural: HGVs, CVs.

The first time you use an abbreviated term, write it out in full followed by the abbreviation or acronym in brackets. This isn't necessary if the abbreviation is so familiar to your audience that it is the more often used and more readily understood form, eg HIV, DNA, MP.

Ampersands (&)

Avoid using an ampersand (&) unless it forms part of a company name:

Procter & Gamble, Marks & Spencer

Don't use it as a general substitute for 'and'.

Apostrophes

Use apostrophes to:

- represent missing letters, eg don't, isn't, Helen's early

- denote periods of time, eg a day's leave, a week's holiday, in three weeks' time

- show possession, eg Jane's bag, the group's project, workers' rights.

For nouns ending in 's', follow these guidelines:

- singular: use the normal 's, eg his boss's car, the business's success

- singular proper nouns: go by sound – in general, use 's for monosyllabic names and ' alone for polysyllabic names, eg James's book, Cass's sister, Emphasis' trainers, Dickens' novels, in Jesus' name (note that biblical and classical names usually take ' alone)

- plural: use ', eg the Joneses' dog, other businesses' problems

- singular in meaning, but plural in form: use ', eg the United States' foreign policy, the Philippines' president.

For joint possession, eg Janet and John's book, use an apostrophe only after the second name. Use an apostrophe after each name, eg David's and Sarah's books, for separate possession, ie each person owns different book(s):

Bill and Nancy's address (they live together).

Bill's and Nancy's addresses (they live apart).

Don't use an apostrophe where 'its' is a possessive pronoun, eg the dog ate its bone. 'It's' is always short for 'it is' or 'it has'. In general, don't use an apostrophe to make a plural, including in dates and abbreviations, eg peas, HGVs, CVs, 1990s. Exceptions arise only where to omit the apostrophe might cause ambiguity, eg the do's and don'ts, A's and B's.

Brackets

Use round brackets to:

- include optional information, eg almost half (48 per cent)

- explain a term, eg upper case (capital letters)

- introduce an abbreviation, eg the summary review memorandum (SRM)

- cross-refer, eg in the plain English dictionary (page 43).

Use square brackets to:

- include an editorial comment or direction, eg a huge bonus [Rob, please confirm]

- include a clarification that is not part of quoted text, eg 'The position [in business writing training] is far from clear.'

The full stop should lie inside the closing bracket if the whole sentence is bracketed, and outside if the bracketed section forms only part of the whole sentence:

Hope this helps. (Look at the website too.)

If you'd like more help, get in touch (or look at the website).

Colons

Use colons to:

* introduce lists, eg the three things we need: time, investment and creativity

* introduce bullets

* introduce extracts or long quotes (see *Commas,* page 52, for introducing short quotes)

* emphasise a question, eg The question is: are their business processes up to the job?

* lead the reader from an idea (usually in the form of a statement that could be a complete sentence) to its consequence or logical continuation, eg He was very tired when he did that piece of work: there were lots of mistakes in it.

Compare this final use of the colon, where there is a step forward in argument (often cause: effect, or fact: explanation), with the similar use of the semicolon, which links balanced or parallel clauses (see *Semicolons*, page 55).

Use lower case after a colon, except when introducing a list of bullets that are whole sentences (see *Bullets*, page 41).

Commas

Use commas to:

- help the reader understand the sense of something, eg However, you might feel the new law will make a difference. However you might feel, the new law will make a difference.

- mark the end of a secondary clause that begins a sentence, eg Although it was raining, we decided to go for a picnic.

- show that information is extra to the main idea, eg The photocopier, which is on the second floor, needs repairing.

- separate items in a list, eg She wanted eggs, ham and bacon.

- denote how items are split in lists, eg The sandwiches they stocked were ham, chicken, ham and tomato, and chicken and cucumber.

- introduce short quotes, eg Clara says, 'We need to act quickly.'

Dashes

Use dashes to:

- explain, paraphrase or draw a conclusion from something you have just written, eg He had a natural flair for leadership – hence his promotion.

- highlight a parenthetical point, eg The show – a runaway success – has just had its final week.

- show a range or sequence, eg 1999–2004, A–Z, 5pm–6pm, London–Edinburgh line.

There are two kinds of dash: the em-rule (—) and the en-rule (–). British style typically uses the en-rule; American style typically uses the em-rule. At Emphasis, we use the en-rule. Be sure to put a space either side of it, except when showing range. (American em-rules don't use spaces.)

Don't confuse an en-rule with a hyphen: it is twice the length (see *Hyphens*, opposite).

Exclamation marks

Use exclamation marks sparingly and singly to express surprise, shock or despair, eg I don't believe it!

Do not use them to add excitement to dull writing. It doesn't work.

Full stops

Use plenty. And put a single space after a full stop.

Hyphens

Use hyphens to:

- join words in adjectival phrases before the noun, ie where the words work together to describe something, eg information-led society, long-term solution (but not if the first word ends in -ly, eg highly prized author)

- add the prefix 're' only when 're' means 'again' and only when omitting the hyphen would cause confusion with another word, eg re-sign/resign

- form some compound words.

At Emphasis, we follow the guidelines below:

One word

breakdown (n)	changeover (n)	cooperate	coordinate
database	email	inbox	laptop
masterclass	ongoing	online	proofread
semicolon	shortlist	website	worldwide

Hyphenated

cost-effective	decision-maker	eye-opener
full-time	high-impact writing	in-house course
job-share	like-minded	self-assured
set-up (n)	spell-check	top-up (n)
up-to-date version	year-end review	

Separate words

| break down (v) | line manager | per cent |
| set up (v) | version that is up to date | web page |

Question marks

Use question marks for direct questions, eg What are we going to do?

Don't use them for sentences such as: I wonder if you could let me know.

Quotation marks

Use single quotation marks for direct speech and for highlighting words or phrases. Use double quotation marks only for a quote within a quote. Introduce short quotes with a comma (see *Commas*, page 52) and long quotes with a colon (see *Colons*, page 51).

Put the punctuation within the quotation marks only if it's part of the quote. Quoting a complete sentence means quoting the full stop too. So it goes inside the quotation marks. But quoting part of the sentence doesn't, so the full stop goes outside. The following examples illustrate most eventualities:

She said, 'The food wasn't even hot.'

She said, 'The food wasn't even hot and all the manager could say was, "Better eat it quickly then," which wasn't very helpful.'

'I will not be coming back,' she said, 'even if they beg me.'

'I will not', she repeated, 'be coming back.'

How many people said, 'We're not coming back'?

She asked, 'Are you coming back?'

Did she ask, 'Are you coming back?'

Semicolons

Think of semicolons as 'super commas'. Use them to:

* separate long phrases in a list when at least one of the phrases contains a comma, eg You will need the following items: climbing boots (or strong walking shoes); two pairs of lightweight trousers; and – most importantly – a waterproof jacket, which must have zipped internal pockets.

* link two related clauses that could otherwise be joined with 'and' or 'but', eg Some people do their best work in the morning; others are at their best in the afternoon.

The chief virtue that
language can have
is clarity.

Hippocrates

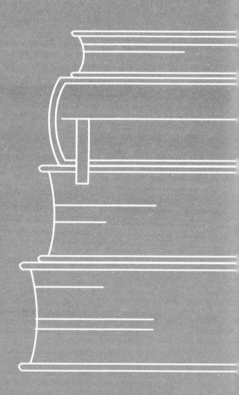

7

Problem words

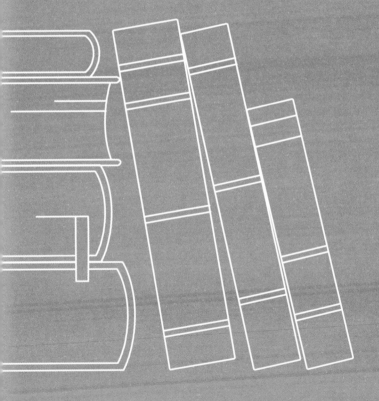

This chapter deals with words that are commonly misused, misspelt or otherwise abused. If you can't find what you're looking for anywhere else in this guide, look here.

affect/effect

Both are commonly used as verbs but mean different things. To affect means 'to influence' or 'to adopt a pose, assume the manner of' (as in 'affectation'):

This weather affected my mood; he affected indifference.

To effect means 'to bring about' or 'accomplish':

The council effected a change to the rubbish collection rota.

Only 'effect' is commonly used as a noun ('affect' as a noun relates to emotional state and is used only in a narrow psychological context):

The effects of the hurricane were felt across the island.

among/amongst

Use 'among'.

anyone/any one

One word when referring to a person, eg Is anyone there? Otherwise, two words, eg He received three job offers, any one of which would have suited him.

centre on/around

Use 'centre on' and 'revolve around'.

compare to/with

Use 'compare to' to liken things, eg Shall I compare thee to a summer's day?; He compared Jenny to her mum. (He felt Jenny to be similar to her mum.)

Use 'compare with' to consider similarities or differences, eg He compared Jenny with her mum. (He assessed the two women's relative merits.)

complement/ compliment

The first means 'to support, make whole or expand', eg This project complements the work we did last year. The second means 'to encourage or praise', eg He complimented Jenny.

Likewise, 'complimentary' and 'complementary' have different meanings. Complementary therapy supports or broadens existing treatment; complimentary treatment is free.

comprise

No 'of' with 'comprise', eg The group comprises a trainer, an accountant and a salesperson.

Or try 'consists of' instead, eg The group consists of a trainer, an accountant and a salesperson.

continual/continuous

A continual buzzing is a noise that happens repeatedly but not constantly. Continuous buzzing doesn't stop.

data

Treat 'data' as singular, eg Send me this data (not these data). Technically 'data' is plural, as is 'agenda'. But nobody uses the singular 'agendum', and the singular 'datum' likewise comes across as pedantic.

dependant/dependent

Your dependants are the ones who depend on you, such as your family. Dependent means 'contingent upon', eg The contract renewal is dependent on your performance.

disinterested/ uninterested

If you're disinterested in something, you are impartial and have no stake in the outcome. If you're uninterested, you simply couldn't care less.

fewer/less

Use 'fewer' for countable things and 'less' for uncountable things, eg There are fewer bottles but less milk.

Sometimes the boundaries are blurred, eg It is less than ten miles to London. Here, the ten miles is thought of as one total distance, rather than ten units of one mile. Apply common sense if in doubt.

focusing/focussing

Both are correct. Use the version with one 's'.

'h' at the beginning of a word

Use 'an' before a word beginning with a silent 'h', eg 'an hour', but 'a hostage' and 'a hotel'.

however

Punctuation around 'however' depends on how you use it. Where it is an aside, put commas around it. However, if it starts a new point (as it does here), it must follow a full stop or semicolon and not a comma. Consider these examples:

These things, however, are bound to happen.

These things are bound to happen; however, we must find a solution.

However, these things are bound to happen.

However these things happen, we must find a solution.

-ise/-ize

Use the standard British convention of -ise where there's a choice, eg realise, organise, apologise.

lead/led

The regular past tense and past participle of 'to lead' is 'led', not 'lead'. 'Lead' (as a noun) is what you used to find in a pencil or a piece of piping.

momentarily

In UK English, this means 'for a moment', eg I momentarily lost my bearings. In US English, momentarily commonly means 'at any moment', eg I'll finish this momentarily. Stick to the UK version.

practice/practise

In UK English, 'practice' is the noun, 'practise' the verb, eg I need to do my piano practice, because I need to practise playing the piano.

presently

This means 'soon', not 'at present'.

principal/principle

'Principal' is a noun or adjective that means 'main' or 'chief', eg the principal of the college; the principal point. 'Principle' is a noun that means 'fundamental characteristic, belief or doctrine', eg the principle of free speech.

supersede

Spelt with an 's' not a 'c'.

that/which

In general, use 'that' to define and 'which' to explain or inform:

The report that was published last year was excellent.

Here, 'that' defines the report we're talking about, ie the one that was published last year, not the one that was published the year before.

The report, which was published last year, has been accepted.

Here, 'which' introduces information not central to the meaning of the sentence: we could remove the middle section and it would still make sense, just as we could if it were in brackets.

So 'which' qualifies and usually follows a comma.

while/whilst

Use 'while'.

Index

Page numbers in bold show
where the subject is explored
in more depth

Abbreviations 10, 46, **48**, 50
 use when writing for a global
 audience 34

Acronyms 10, **48**
 use when writing for a global
 audience 34

Active voice **9**, 13, 23

Ampersands 49

Apostrophes 47, 48, **49**

Audience, writing for a global 33–37

Bold 42

Brackets 48, **50**, 62

Brand names **43**

Bullets **41**, 51

Capital letters 42, **44–45**, 48

Captions 42

Colloquialisms 35

Colons 41, 42, 48, **51**, 55

Commas 45, 46, 48, **52**, 55, 60, 62

Cultures, writing for different 28,
33–37

Dashes 47, **52**

Dates, how to write 47

Editing 6, **10**, 13

Email
 attachments **27**, 28
 subject lines 27
 tips on writing 25–29

Em-rule 52

En-rule 47, **52**

Exclamation marks 53

Extracts **42**, 51

Fonts 41

Full stops 20, 41, 48, 50, **53**, 55, 60

Grammar 9

Headings **40**, 42

House style 39–55

Hyperlinks **18–19**

Hyphens 46, 47, **53**, 54

Italics 43

Jargon 10, 30, 31

Jargon buster 30–31

Keywords 18

Layout 18, **40**

Lists 41, 51, **52**

Lower case 41, **44**, **45**, 51

Management-speak 11, 30

Nouns 10, 11, 49, 53, 58, 61

Numbers, writing 46–47

Paragraphs
    length 12, 13
    use when writing for the web 20

Passive voice 9

Percentages 47

Planning your writing 6

Problem words 57–62

Proofreading
    tips on 13
    when writing emails 29

Punctuation 41, 45, **48–55**, 60

Question marks 54

Quotation marks 55

Quotes 42, 51, 52, **55**

Readability principles **7–13**, 20
    be direct **8**, 23
    use the active voice **9**, 23
    keep it short and simple **10–11**, 28, 37
    stick to one sentence, one idea 12
    check it! 13

Reader-centred writing **6–7**, 13, 16

Semicolons 51, **55**, 60

Style
    email writing 28
    house 39–55
    writing 7

Spelling 57–62

Subheads 6, 13, 18, 20, 28, **40**, 42
    use when writing for the web 18

Tables 42

Tips
  clear writing 5–13
  proofreading 13
  writing for a global audience
  33–37

Underlining 42
  use when writing for the web 19

Upper case 29, **44–45**

Verbs 10, 11, 37, 58, 61

Web, writing for the 15–23

Website visitors **16–17**, 18

Writing training 66

Who are we?

At Emphasis, we know that business writing is something that, worldwide, millions of people struggle with. So we've made it our mission to help them.

Since 1998, we've helped more than 50,000 people write better documents, email and web content – mainly through the 5,000 courses that we've run for organisations across the globe.

Because we're specialists, we can create bespoke in-company courses in any area of written communication, from how to reply to a complaint email through to how to write a bid for a national rail franchise. Our in-house team of experts includes specialists in report writing, preparing speeches for senior executives and writing English for speakers of other languages.

We work with a huge range of organisations in the public and private sectors. These include government departments and agencies, such as the Home Office, the Cabinet Office, HMRC, the Environment Agency, Natural England and Dstl; household names, including M&S, Nestlé, Coca-Cola, Royal Mail and Warner Bros; and major professional-services firms, such as EY, PwC, KPMG, Deloitte, Grant Thornton, Accenture, Slaughter and May, and Linklaters. We also work with much smaller organisations – and with individuals – through our regular public courses.

To find out more, go to **www.writing-skills.com**, where you can get more advice on how to transform your writing at work.